English Electric Traction
Chester to Holyhead

Volume 1: 1959 to 1983

Contents

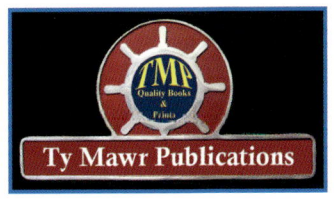

Ty Mawr Publications

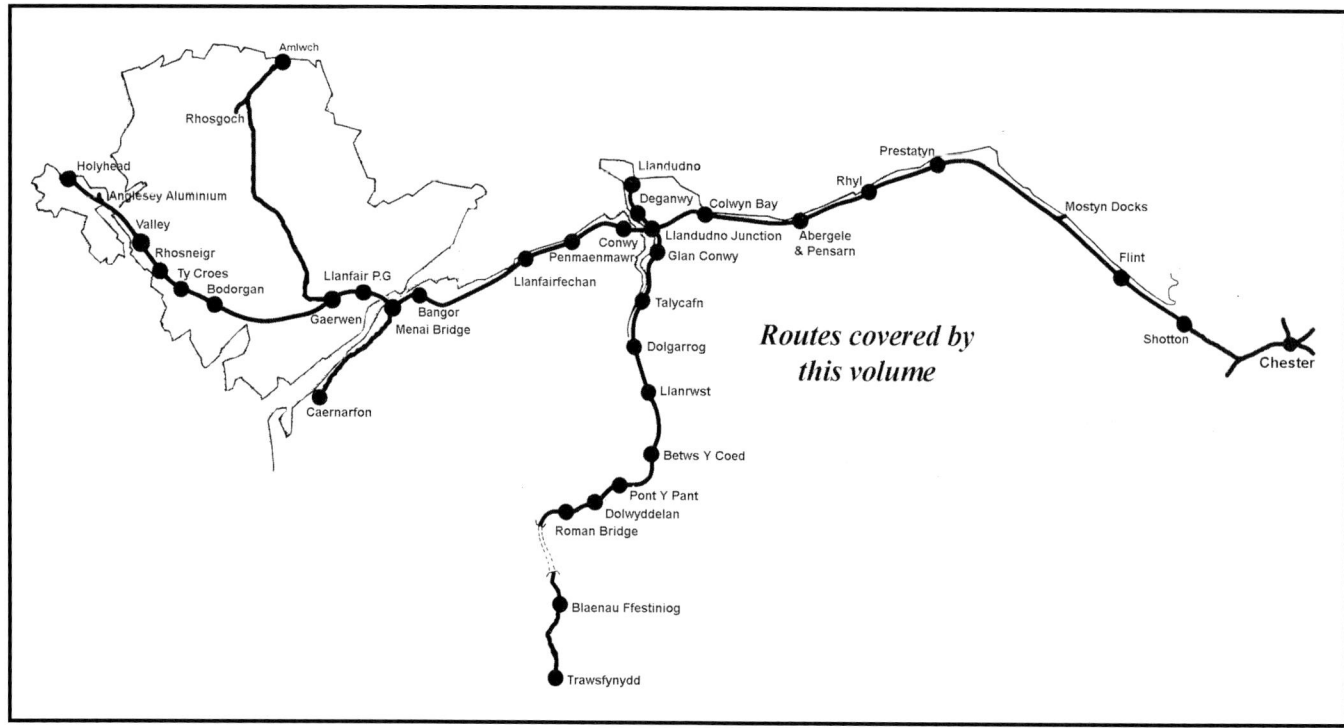

Routes covered by this volume

Published by

**Ty Mawr Publications
Holmes Chapel
Cheshire
UK**
www.tymawrpublications.co.uk

© 2011 Steve Morris

ISBN 0-9552354-5-6
978-0-9552354-5-0

Design & typesetting by
Steve Morris

Front cover
40184 at the head of a ballast train from Penmaenmawr sits alongside 40087 on the 12.15 Holyhead to Crewe service. Rhyl, July 21st 1981. **Photo Steve Morris.**

Back cover top left
Class 20 number D8036 (20036) is seen departing Llandudno Junction on a working to Blaenau Ffestiniog conveying a transformer for use in a Hydro Electric scheme, the first visit of a class 20 to North Wales. February 19th 1961. **Photo BR LMR.**

Back cover top right
9th April 1983 and 37165 heads an additional container train bound for Felixstowe out of Holyhead, a very rare working for the class at the time. **Photo Steve Morris.**

Back cover middle left
28th June 1980, Mostyn Dock footbridge. 40070 heads 1A56, 12.57 Holyhead to Euston working, the second lunchtime boat-train in the summer months. **Photo Peter Hanahoe.**

Back cover middle right
An unidentified class 50 heads a Llandudno to Birmingham service through Llandudno Junction during the summer of 1976, one of the last 1970's class 50 sightings in North Wales. **Photo Larry Davies.**

Back cover bottom
Gas Turbine locomotive "GT3" seen on test at Llandudno Junction in March 1961.
Photo Peter Owen.

Acknowledgements
I am indebted to a number of people who have provided images and information used in this publication. In particular to Norman Kneale, Barry Wynne, Peter Owen and Wyn Hobson who recorded early Diesel workings during a time when most people were concentrating on the departure of Steam. To Peter Hanahoe, Ron Watson-Jones, Dave "Trains" Williams, Dave Rapson and Pat Webb for their invaluable assistance and last but not least to Sue, Matt and Jack for their patience throughout the production process.
I hope this publication serves as a reminder to the reader of the service provided by these British built products during a period that was dominated by locomotive haulage, an era that will never be repeated. Please feel free to drop me a line via the Ty Mawr Publications website with any comments, corrections or otherwise!
Steve Morris, Holmes Chapel, August 2011.
www.tymawrpublications.co.uk

References
"The Allocation History of BR Diesels and Electrics" parts 1 to 5 by Roger Harris.
2D53 website by Dave Plimmer. www.2d53.co.uk
Class 40 Motherlist by Alan Wilson. www.itsa40.co.uk

INTRODUCTION

Welcome to the first of two volumes celebrating over fifty years continuous service for English Electric built Diesel locomotives on the route between Chester and Holyhead. This publication covers the period between the first sighting of "EE" traction on the route in 1959, through to 1983. I have made the decision to include only those mainline locomotive classes produced by English Electric. This means classes 20, 37, 40 and 50, although class 55's will also feature in volume two. Non "EE" products but fitted with their power units do not feature, so, class 31's and, perhaps a little tenuously, 56's (volume 2), have been left out.

It was as early as 8th August 1959 when brand new class 40 D222 (40022) worked from Crewe to Llandudno and back, probably the first Diesel hauled service in North Wales. D233 (40033) was allocated to Holyhead for driver training in October of the same year which subsequently led to the Dieselisation of "Irish Mail" and "Emerald Isle Express" duties to and from London Euston on April 25th 1960.

Above. Brand new D233 seen stabled at Holyhead during driver training duties in October 1959.
Photo John Cave MBE.

During the period covered by this volume, "EE" traction in North Wales was mainly represented by class 40's. They monopolised Diesel hauled passenger workings throughout the 1960's although they did hand a number of these over to newly built class 47's from 1965 onwards. However, they remained in widespread use throughout the 1970's and into the 80's, mainly on secondary passenger services to and from Manchester and Crewe, and summer dated services from Yorkshire and The Midlands in and out of Llandudno. In addition, following the closure of Holyhead shed to steam in December 1966 they took over a large number of through freight and other non passenger workings such as those conveying containers, petroleum based products, parcels and newspapers. From the early 1980's onwards, following reduced use of the class in general on passenger duties and the rundown of the fleet, they were also used on local Trip workings as well as chemical traffic to and from Amlwch. The class 40 proved to be a reliable and versatile provider of motive power and particularly suited to the North Wales Coast route.

The second type to appear in the area was the class 20. This was as early as February 1961 when D8036 (20036) worked an out of gauge load conveying a transformer to Blaenau Ffestiniog. There was then a gap of over 18 years before the class returned, this time working a passenger charter to Blaenau Ffestiniog during the Conwy Valley line Centenary celebrations. 20153/165 were used, the date being July 22nd 1979. That was it as far as this volume is concerned, the next recorded working not taking place until the summer of 1985.

Class 50's arrived on the scene in 1967 and would become the second most popular "EE" product to work the route during the period in question. Initially, having just been delivered from Vulcan Foundry, they were seen working light engine to and from Rhyl on commissioning runs from Crewe. D400 was the first to be recorded making three runs on the 4th, 5th and 6th of October 1967. Arrival time was normally between 10 and 11 in the morning with a return as soon as a path became available. These trips were repeated by a number of the fleet during the build programme which lasted until the end of 1968. Following introduction to traffic they started to appear piloting class 40's or 47's on running in turns from Crewe works after overhaul. This normally involved the 09.35 Euston to Bangor or 10.20 Euston to Llandudno which returned at 15.10 in both cases, both of the Diesels having taken over from Electric traction at Crewe. In the early 1970's the odd appearance on routine passenger workings across "The Coast" started. These were more frequent following completion of the electrification of the West Coast mainline north of Weaver Junction in May 1974. Between the summer of 1974 and 1976 this resulted in a number of regular appearances for the class on passenger duties between Crewe and Holyhead (19.15 down Euston and 00.55 return) and the 4D62 Willesden Freightliner. The final appearance as far west as Holyhead during the period covered by this volume, and in fact during regular service for the fleet as a whole, was on 11/12th June 1976 when 50046 worked the "19.15/00.55" passenger diagram. Volume two will cover several other visits on charters or whilst on test runs for preserved members of the fleet.

Last but not least, class 37's made spasmodic appearances from 1968 onwards. The first reported sighting was on June 23rd 1968 when two pairs of Tinsley based examples, D6806/09 (37106/109) and D6807/11 (37107/111), worked BR employee specials from the Sheffield area to Rhyl. There was also a reported working to Anglesey Aluminium on the petroleum coke service during 1972 followed by 37283 at the head of 1E93 the 09.00 Llandudno to York on June 3rd 1978. Next came 37055, again on 'the coke' on November 5th 1981 and 37165 on a special container train in and out of Holyhead on April 8th 1983. This was closely followed by 37173 on May 6th 1983 on another container train to Holyhead before rescuing failed 47481 on the 19.25 from Bangor to Manchester. This was the first class 37 worked passenger service west of Llandudno Junction and a sign of things to come! The final sighting during this period was of 37131 during the evening of November 17th 1983 whilst working a track train to Llandudno Junction.

1.
Chester to Rhyl

English Electric produced the first Diesels to be used in North Wales. They could be seen in action on the Chester to Rhyl section of the line to Holyhead from 1959 onwards. Class 40's saw regular use on passenger and a variety of freight services throughout the period covered by this volume. The second most common type was the class 50 with early workings involving commissioning runs to Rhyl when brand new from Vulcan Foundry during 1967 and 1968. As mentioned in the introduction, the odd class 37 also worked along the section during the period and as will be seen later, class 20's visited the area twice.

At the beginning of each chapter in this volume we will take a look at the route as it was during the period which it covers. On leaving Chester station the line passes a Depot on the right, home to many a class 40 between duties, then the junction for Birkenhead, also on the right, before running through tunnels under the line to Chester Northgate station (closed in 1969) and the City walls prior to crossing Roodee Viaduct over the river Dee. This is followed by Saltney Junction, the line to Wrexham and Shrewsbury branching off to the left, then Mold Junction yard, host to a number of class 40 hauled freight workings throughout the period. The line continues onwards through Shotton without any major gradients to tackle, the once busy John Summers, later British Steel, complex visible across the river Dee. Next comes Connah's Quay, home to the Crumps wagon works, before Flint. Bagillt marks the start of a four track section that, until the late 1960's, ran almost to Llandudno Junction to cope with the huge volume of summer holiday traffic, a large proportion of which was in the hands of class 40's from the mid 1960's onwards. A few miles on is the Courtaulds factory at Greenfield, served by a range of freight services throughout the period, a number class 40 hauled. Holywell Junction comes next, then Mostyn, home to a dock complex on the river Dee. Point of Ayr colliery is the last industrial site on the Chester to Rhyl section before the line heads along the coast through Prestatyn and the junction for the Dyserth branch (closed 1973). Finally, the route runs between the sea and numerous caravan parks before reaching Rhyl where during the 1960's trains often had to queue up to enter the station on a busy summer Saturday. At the start of the period covered by this volume over 50 down trains were sometimes scheduled to reach Rhyl in a three hour period on such a day, how times have changed!

Above
Two for the price of one! Class 40 No 306, later 40106, the unique green liveried member of the class, is seen with ex works class 50 No 417 (50017) on a return running in turn from Bangor, probably the 15.10 to Euston. The fact that the class 40 is leading suggests that all is not well with 417. Both locomotives would be removed at Crewe in favour of electric traction. Date, 23rd March 1973.
Photo Ian Langhorn. www.the-transport-photo-interchange.co.uk.

Right
A Holyhead bound Freightliner is captured passing through Chester behind class 40 number 214 (40014) "Antonia" on May 9th 1972. The A bank side nameplate is already missing by now.

Below
Class 50 number 409 (50009) approaches Chester on an extra up working on March 19th 1972.

Photos Ian Langhorn.
www.the-transport-photo-interchange.co.uk

Below
May 13th 1977 and 40022 is seen sitting at the back of Chester depot in an area called Brook Lane. Behind the loco there are two wrought iron bridge girders that had recently been removed from where they had carried tracks into a banana warehouse at the old Chester Northgate station.
They were subsequently given a new lease of life spanning the river Tygwyn north of Harlech following renovation in Welshpool.
Named "Laconia" in 1962, 40022 remained in traffic until withdrawal from Carlisle Kingmoor in March 1984. Cutting would follow at Doncaster works during October of the same year.
Photo Dave Plimmer.

Above
Longsight based 40055 runs through the centre road at Chester heading the 4D62 Willesden to Holyhead Freightliner on March 29th 1982. During this period there would be up to four Freightliner workings into Holyhead port every 24 hours from terminals at Crewe, Birmingham Lawley Street, Manchester Trafford Park and Willesden respectively. 40055 would only remain in traffic for a further 8 months and following a period in store at Reddish depot was disposed of at Doncaster works during May 1983.
Photo Steve Morris.

Above
40065 and a dead 40036 head the 14.18 Crewe to Holyhead at Chester on August 29th 1981. They had worked in tandem from Crewe but "036" was shut down on arrival at Chester.
Until a few months prior to this, 40065 would have been an extremely rare visitor to the area having been Haymarket based since new in March 1960. She would however only remain in traffic a few weeks longer being withdrawn in early November.　　**Photo John Stephens.**

Right
40076 approaches Chester station en route Holyhead on the daily Freightliner working from Trafford Park during early 1982. Due Holyhead at just after 8pm, the return service was just after 5am the next day.
Photo Steve Morris.

Left
May 21st 1972. Gateshead based 345 (40145) approaches Chester station past number 4 signal box.
Withdrawn in May 1983 as a result of derailment damage, 40145 was later purchased by the Class Forty Preservation Society and became the first, and at the time of writing, only member of the class to return to mainline operation when she returned to North Wales on "The Christmas Cracker" railtour to Holyhead on the 30th of November 2002.
Photo Ian Langhorn.
www.the-transport-photo-interchange.co.uk

Above
40015 "Aquitania" arrives at Chester on 1K29, the 12.07 Holyhead to Crewe. The stencilled nameplate provided by Ron Watson-Jones is clearly visible. Date, March 5th 1983.
Right
Saturday July 9th 1983 and 40050 is seen on the approach to Chester City Walls on an extra up Freightliner from Holyhead. Withdrawal would come within a month of this date before despatch to Doncaster works and being rapidly broken up by November, almost 24 years since being built.
Photos Peter Hanahoe.

Above
40113 bursts into life just outside Chester whilst working the 1D32, 10.29 Birmingham New Street to Holyhead on August 4th 1979. Withdrawn from service in October 1981 the end would come at Swindon works by January 1984.
Photo Dave Rapson.

Below
July 21st 1975 and celebrity green liveried 40106 is seen at Saltney heading 7F60, a ballast working from Penmaenmawr to St Helens. A visit to Crewe works in 1978 resulted in another coat of green paint meaning that "106" never carried blue livery. **Photo Dave Rapson.**

Above

Mold Junction, April 24th 1978. 40181 is seen heading towards Chester on 6E36, the 05.50 Holyhead RTZ to Humber refinery petroleum coke empties. This flow was covered by a dedicated fleet of 17 "PAB" 46t hoppers that were build specifically for the job by Doncaster works in 1970/71, the coke being used in the production of anodes used in the Aluminium smelting process. They operated until the traffic was lost to sea in 2001 following a fire at the Immingham Conoco refinery in April of that year. Following several years in store they were cut up at Locks scrap yard in Bangor during February 2008. Smelting has since ceased at the Holyhead plant.   **Photo Dave Rapson.**

Below

385 (40185) passes Hawarden airport working a Willesden to Holyhead Freightliner on July 19th 1973. Introduced to York depot in March 1962, this particular example would remain in service until August 7th 1983 with withdrawal coming from Carlisle Kingmoor. The final trip to Doncaster works was made in the company of sister loco 40184 in September 1983. Both were broken up swiftly by the end of the year.
Photo Wyn Hobson.

Above
40082 hauls a dead 40030 towards Shotton station on 1K28, the 09.25 Holyhead to Crewe on September 6th 1980. The cooling towers of Connah's Quay power station can be seen in the background.
Photo Peter Hanahoe.

Below
Longsight based 40112 heads through Shotton whilst working 2D99, the 15.32 Manchester Victoria to Bangor on September 1st 1978. An early candidate for withdrawal, the end for "112" would come in December 1980.
Photo Dave Rapson.

Above
May 14th 1979. 40110 thunders through Shotton Low Level station on 4H59, the 05.34 Holyhead to Trafford Park Freightliner. Until 1978 this service also conveyed a portion for Lawley Street that was detached at Mold Junction. By 1979 traffic levels justified the introduction of a through working to the Birmingham terminal. **Photo Dave Rapson**.

Below
Shotton Low level again and 40133 is seen working 6F31, 12.20 Penmaenmawr quarry to St Helens on September 5th 1979. New to Crewe North in February 1961, this particular example would remain an "LMR" loco throughout its life with withdrawal from Longsight depot coming in January 1984. **Photo Dave Rapson.**

Above
40028 "Samaria" approaches Shotton on 4H60, the Mondays Only 05.28 Holyhead to Trafford Park "Liner" on July 24th 1978. Introduced in August 1959, this example would have a relatively long life, withdrawal not coming until October 1984 after over 25 years service.

Left
19th September 1979 and 40170 is seen nearing Shotton Low Level heading for Manchester Victoria working 2J99, the 11.30 departure from Bangor.

Photos Dave Rapson.

Right
40028 again!
This time she is working 4G66, the 05.51 Holyhead to Lawley Street container service. It is seen passing the entrance to the CC Crumps wagon works at Connah's Quay. These trains were well loaded and just over a quarter mile in length.
Date, June 8th 1979.
Photo Dave Rapson.

Above
Connah's Quay, July 3rd 1979.
40016 "Campania" complete with
a good dose of nose end door
damage is seen heading 2D99, the
15.40 Bangor to Manchester.

Left
40107 departs Flint station on a
Bangor to Manchester working.
The date is August 30th 1979 and
an industrial backdrop dominates
the skyline, all gone by the present
day of course! Interestingly "107"
spent a period in store at Horwich
works prior to an overhaul at
Crewe works in August 1980.
However, the reprieve did not last
long with final withdrawal coming
by December 1981.
Photos Dave Rapson.

Right
Bagillt, March 1st 1976.
Until July 1985 the Courtaulds
complex at Greenfield received
regular consignments of fuel oil
by rail. This one, headed by
40091, is 6D40, a 13.06 departure
from Brunswick terminal.
This was located on the former
Cheshire Lines route from
Liverpool Central to Manchester
Central. Other flows to the site
originated from Robeston and
Herbrandston in South Wales.
40091 would be the last class 40
to be cut up, being dealt with at
Crewe works in December 1988.
Photo Dave Rapson.

Above
August 28th 1979 and Haymarket based 40165 has found itself on the 15.40 Manchester to Bangor, seen departing Flint station. This was an exceptionally rare working for this example and was followed by the 19.30 return. She was back in North Wales on the 30th working the 17.18 Llandudno to Manchester.
Photo Dave Rapson.

Below
With the Courtaulds industrial complex dominating the skyline, 40019 "Caronia" rushes through Greenfield working 1J30, the 11.03 Bangor to Manchester on October 27th 1981. A rake of oil tanks can be seen parked in the unloading siding adjacent to the down line.
Photo Dave Rapson.

Right
September 6th 1982. 40015 "Aquitania" speeds past Mostyn Docks on the 1J30 Bangor to Manchester. An assortment of wagons are present in the dock sidings, including several full of sulphur waiting movement to the Octel plant at Amlwch. New to Willesden in June 1959, 40015 would remain based on the "LM" throughout her life of over 25 years. Withdrawal came from Longsight in November 1984 before being cut up at Swindon works two years later.
Photo Peter Hanahoe.

Left
By the 1980's, class 40 running in turns were becoming less common. This one taken at Mostyn Docks on June 28th 1980 was even more unusual in that it was on a Saturday. Ex works 40150 is seen heading 1D11, the 11.18 Crewe to Llandudno with Healey Mills based 40049 tucked inside as insurance. This would be 150's final classified repair and she would go on to be one of the last class 40's in service, surviving right up until January 22nd 1985 prior to withdrawal at Crewe after a light engine move from Oxley.
Photo Dave Trains.

Right
A rare daytime class 50 working in North Wales is captured on May 26th 1975. 50035 is seen on a down additional service near Prestatyn. This particular example would be one of the final batch of class 50's to be transferred away from Crewe, heading for Bristol Bath Road in January 1976.
Following withdrawal in 1990, the then "Ark Royal" became the first of the class to enter preservation following purchase by The Fifty Fund. At the time of writing she is based at Kidderminster on the Severn Valley Railway.
Photo Trefor Thompson.

Above
June 20th 1981. Gateshead based 40187 erupts as she passes Mostyn at the head of 2D82, the 09.15 Liverpool to Llandudno. Withdrawn in August the following year, this example ended its days at Doncaster works in June 1985.
Photo Peter Hanahoe.

Below
40174 approaches Prestatyn station on the 4D59, 11.12 Saturday Only Trafford Park to Holyhead Freightliner on July 12th 1980. Withdrawn from Longsight in May 1984, "174" was cut up at the same place as 40187 above, but some six months earlier. **Photo Peter Hanahoe.**

Above
August 28th 1982 and Healey Mills based 40092 slows for the stop at Prestatyn station whilst heading the 09.00 Llandudno to York. A transfer to Longsight would take place two months later but withdrawal followed within weeks of this taking place.

Left
40135 approaches Prestatyn on the weekly petroleum coke flow from the Humber oil refinery to the Anglesey Aluminium RTZ plant near Holyhead on July 12th 1980. Withdrawn in December 1986 after a period in departmental service, 40135 became the second class 40 to be preserved by the CFPS and is currently based on the East Lancashire Railway at Bury.
Photos Peter Hanahoe.

Right
July 4th 1981. 40065 accelerates out of Prestatyn station heading for York on 1E86, the 09.00 departure from Llandudno. Only a few more months service remained for "065", withdrawal coming in November of this year. There then followed a period in store at Reddish depot until transfer to Crewe works for disposal, something that was completed by March 1985.
Photo Peter Hanahoe.

Above
40080 passes Dyserth Bay Prestatyn heading 1Z99 conveying the Chester breakdown vans to Llandudno Junction to deal with a minor derailment.
August 28th 1982. **Photo Peter Hanahoe.**

Below
Pioneer 40122 departs Prestatyn on May 23rd 1981 heading for Crewe on 1K28, the 09.23 departure from Holyhead. Withdrawn on August 23rd of this year she would be reinstated on April 24th 1983 prior to overhaul at Toton for use on railtours etc. There then followed almost five years further service before final withdrawal and handing over to the National Railway Museum on April 16th 1988. **Photo Peter Hanahoe.**

2.
Rhyl to Llandudno Junction

Rhyl was one of North Wales' most popular resorts and particularly busy during summer months, especially up to the early 1970's, with the volume of passenger traffic mentioned at the end of the previous chapter reflecting this. The station boasted two through roads and during the period in question had two signal boxes to control the area and associated sidings.

Leaving Rhyl the line runs alongside Marine Lake and its miniature railway to the right before crossing the River Clwyd and Foryd Junction where the line for Denbigh branches off to the left (closed in 1968). Holiday parks then line the route onwards through Abergele and Pensarn before the first real climb since Chester, up the 1 in 100 gradient to Llandulas and on up to the summit located at the entrance to the 485 yard long Penmaenrhos tunnel. After emerging from the tunnel there is a downhill run along the coast with superb views out towards Llandudno before reaching the popular resort of Colwyn Bay. There then follows a short flat section, sweeping around to where the line to Blaenau Ffestiniog and on to Trawsfynydd branches off to the left just before reaching Llandudno Junction. This is home to a depot, marshalling yard and a carriage servicing facilities, a regular haunt for English Electric class 40 locomotives. Early "EE" visitors to Llandudno Junction during 1961 included class 20 D8036, see page 34, and the experimental Gas Turbine locomotive "GT3" which was involved in early trial running along the North Wales Coast, see page 29.

Above
40167 storms out of Rhyl on July 25th 1981 whilst working the summer Saturday 1M08 07.52 Leeds to Llandudno. Introduced to Haymarket in November 1961 as D367, this particular class 40 would remain based there for almost 20 years until a transfer south to Carlisle Kingmoor just before this image was recorded. Sightings of "Scottish" 40's in North Wales were rare and only normally occurred during running in turns from Crewe works or occasionally on services from Manchester or Yorkshire such as this one. However, from the summer of 1981 onwards other ex Scottish 40's would become regular visitors to the area after being transferred South. Examples included 40060/062/065/158/162, all of which were transferred away from Haymarket by the end of July 1981. 40167 was the last of the class to receive a classified repair at Crewe works, during February 1981. Withdrawn from Longsight three years later she would end her days in Doncaster works by the end of May 1984.
Photo Peter Hanahoe.

226 (40026) passes Rhyl number 2 signal box on an up Euston service on July 30th 1972. Although it was planned to name her 'Media', this was cancelled after an objection from the shipping company concerned. The plates themselves still exist although there is debate as to whether they were actually fitted for a short time or not. New to Crewe North in August 1959, 40026 would have a service life of just over 20 years, withdrawal coming from Longsight in April 1980.
Photo S Morris collection.

Above
Healey Mills based 40102 departs Rhyl on August 3rd 1974 heading for Llandudno. This particular locomotive would be amongst the first batch of class 40's to be withdrawn from service as "life expired". This took place as early as January 1976 after a service life of just a little over 15 years! **Photo S Morris collection.**

Right
217 (40027) "Parthia" at Kinmel Bay on the outskirts of Rhyl heads for Holyhead on the 08.15 boat-train from Euston. This was the first time this summer dated service had run since the closure of the Britannia Bridge after the May 1970 fire.
Photo Wyn Hobson.

Above
Whilst booked for a class 47, the occasional class 40 deputised on 1D53, the 10.25 Euston to Llandudno. This summer Saturday dated service was the first to bring rakes of MK3 coaches to North Wales, clearly not a job for a non ETH fitted loco! One such example can be seen at Rhyl on June 27th 1981 behind Gateshead based 40057, a rare combination indeed!
Photo Peter Hanahoe.

Below
July 18th 1981. Displaying an inappropriate headcode, 40166 passes Kinmel Bay, Rhyl, on an up ballast working from Penmaenmawr. This particular loco spent the first 16 years or so of its life based at Haymarket with a transfer south to Longsight in May 1978 where it would remain until ending its days in February 1982.
Photo Peter Hanahoe.

Above
Abergele, June 4th 1983. 40168 is seen heading a Trafford Park to Holyhead "Liner". Along with 40061/063/101/157, this was one of the last five class 40's to be based in Scotland, all being transferred from Haymarket in October 1981.
Photo Peter Hanahoe.

Below
Healey Mills based 40074 slows for a stop at Abergele and Pensarn whilst working 1J30, the 11.30 Bangor to Manchester. Date, May 23rd 1981.
Photo Peter Hanahoe.

Above
1M71, the 09.00 York to Llandudno bursts out of Penmaenrhos
tunnel near Old Colwyn behind 40185 on July 3rd 1982.
Photo Peter Hanahoe.

Below
With works associated with the rebuilding of the A55 road
in full swing, 40056 heads an up working at Old Colwyn in
July 1982.
Photo Peter Hanahoe.

Above
An up extra Freightliner climbs up the 1 in 100 gradient towards Penmaenrhos tunnel behind Longsight based 40047 on Friday July 8th 1983. Unusually, this example of the class ended its days at Toton depot in November 1984 following a brake fault.
Photo Peter Hanahoe.

Below
40009 is seen on the final approach to Colwyn Bay station at the head of 1M08, the 07.52 Leeds to Llandudno on August 14th 1982. "009" would finish its days on November 7th 1984 with celebrity status as the final "Vacuum Only" brake class member.
Photo Peter Hanahoe.

Left
D336 (40136) approaches Colwyn Bay station on the 09.20 Crewe to Holyhead during the summer of 1961. At this stage she has still to receive small yellow nose end warning panels, something that would soon follow. This particular example was the last of the class to loose its green livery, a repaint into corporate blue not coming until 1978.
Photo E N Kneale/S Morris collection.

Above
Edge Hill based D343 (40143) at Colwyn Bay on the 13.25 Holyhead to Euston in August 1963.
Withdrawn on the final day of regular class 40 service, January 22nd 1985, 40143 would enjoy a service life of almost 24 years.
Photo E N Kneale/S Morris collection.

Right
40027 "Parthia" thunders through Colwyn Bay on a down boat-train for Holyhead. August 8th 1975.
Photo S Morris collection.

Right
Having just been renumbered from 334, ex works 40144 speeds through Old Colwyn heading a relief for Manchester on July 6th 1974. The down working had been a 1D24 09.03 relief from Warrington Bank Quay to Bangor.
Photo S Morris collection.

Left
Included, if nothing else due to its rarity value! Haymarket stalwart 40142 is seen pausing at Colwyn Bay working 1J39, the 17.18 Llandudno to Manchester Victoria. It had worked into the area earlier in the day on the 1M59 09.10 Scarborough to Llandudno.
The date is August 11th 1979 and since transfer to Scotland in May 1974 this particular example would have paid few if any visits to North Wales.
Photo John Stephens.

Right
The Colwyn Bay signalman takes a snack as 40183 slows to call at the station heading 1K38, the 17.37 Llandudno to Stoke-on -Trent. August 5th 1980.
Photo E N Kneale/S Morris collection.

Above
Sporting Ron Watson-Jones' "Irish Mail" headboard, Healey Mills based 40192 accelerates out of Colwyn Bay heading for Holyhead on 1D29, the 10.45 from Manchester Victoria on August 7th 1982. One of the last class 40's to remain in regular service, this example was not withdrawn until January 21st 1985 whilst at Bescot.
Photo Peter Hanahoe.

Below
Having failed in Colwyn Bay station, 47440 is assisted forward on the 11.00 Euston to Holyhead by 40141, the ensemble seen on the outskirts of Colwyn Bay at Mochdre. Failures as a result of low coolant were not uncommon at Colwyn Bay, the heavy cant of the track on the down line often being just enough for the header tank contents to tilt sufficiently to trigger the low coolant level switch! Date, July 4th 1981.   **Photo Ron Watson-Jones.**

Above
July 18th 1981 and 40121 has rescued failed 47473 on 1D53, the 10.25 Euston to Llandudno comprising of MK3 stock. This was the second time in a matter of weeks that a class 40 had ended up on this duty, see page 21.
Photo Peter Hananhoe.

Below
Scheduled to arrive at Bangor at 00.21 Saturday morning, the Friday Only 7D35 cement from Penyffordd had arrived with the discharge valves on the wrong side on April 26th 1983! This resulted in a trip back to Chester to turn on the triangle and in this view 40177 is seen at Llandudno Junction returning it to Bangor the following morning. **Photo Dave Trains.**

Above

During the late 1940's, English Electric started the development of an experimental Gas Turbine locomotive. Rated at 2700hp and built on running gear based on a BR standard class 5 steam locomotive, construction would take ten years, starting in Rugby and ending at Vulcan Foundry works Newton-le-Willows in early 1961. Known as "GT3", the concept was out of date by the time it was released to traffic. However it did spend several years on trial. Whilst much of this was undertaken on the Great Central and West Coast mainlines, an early run took GT3 to Llandudno Junction where she is seen in this rare colour image of the locomotive in North Wales taken during March 1961.

Photo Peter Owen.

Below

Until the late 1980's, class 37 working in North Wales were very rare. A previously unreported working by the class took place during the evening of November 17th 1983 when Healey Mills based 37131 worked a continuous welded rail train to Llandudno Junction. This was only the seventh occasion that the class had appeared in North Wales although there had been two others during this particular year, see pages 42 and 56 for example.

In this view the locomotive in question can be seen just after arrival at "The Junction" prior to returning east light engine.

Photo Ron Watson-Jones.

Above
Two of the first batch of class 40's to enter service during 1958 are seen departing Llandudno Junction on July 31st 1982 after 40004 had failed there whilst heading 1J22, the 13.58 Bangor to Manchester, resulting in 40002 being added. Note 47483 derailed in the background!

Below
The final double headed class 40 hauled service from Holyhead ran on July 30th 1983 with 40196 and 40080 working 1A56, the 13.10 to Euston as far as Crewe. Here it is seen departing Llandudno Junction with plenty of 40 fans on board!
Both photos Dave Trains.

3.
Llandudno to Trawsfynydd

During the period covered by this volume Llandudno was the most popular resort in North Wales, and the volume of passenger traffic serving the town, particularly in the summer months up to the mid to late 1970's reflected this. Possibly the first class 40 working in North Wales took place behind D222 (40022) on a Crewe to Llandudno service in the summer of 1959 and from then on the class was used in increasing numbers on a wide range of workings to and from Yorkshire, the Midlands, Potteries as well as Manchester and London. The first class 37 passenger working west of Rhyl took place in June 1978 when 37283 was sent light engine from Newton Heath to take up the 09.00 Llandudno to York, see page 32. Apart from that, class 40's reigned supreme in North Wales!

The Branch to Blaenau Ffestiniog and Trawsfyndd covered some of the most scenic landscape in the country including the two mile 338 yard tunnel on the approach to Blaenau itself. The construction of Trawsfynydd nuclear power station in the late 1950's resulted in the opening of a connection with the Great Western line to Bala at Blaenau Ffestiniog in 1964 to permit transport of nuclear flasks along the section. Further improvements to the layout including repositioning of Blaenau Ffestiniog station were made in 1981/82 to improve interchange with the Ffestiniog Railway.

The first Diesel locomotive to work along "the branch" was an English Electric product and came as early as 1961 when class 20 D8036 (20036) worked an out of gauge load, see page 34. A further visit by the class came in 1979 during the centenary celebrations for the route. However, the class 40 was the most regularly used "EE" traction along the line. They worked a number of charters and some timetabled services from Llandudno during the summers of 1982/83. Trip workings including the occasional one conveying nuclear flasks became more frequent in the early 1980's, giving the opportunity to see a class 40 working as far as Trawsfynydd.

Above
A reminder of times gone by. 40174 waits to depart Llandudno at the head of a control relief (remember those?) on Sunday July 10th 1983. This was one of several loco hauled workings into Llandudno on this particular day, there was even another control relief hauled by 47454. This would be the last summer of regular class 40 workings along the North Wales Coast and in and out of this resort, class 45's cascaded from the Midland Mainline starting to take over a number of duties.

New to traffic at Camden in January 1962, this particular example of the class would remain based on "LMR" depots for its whole life, withdrawal coming from Longsight depot in May 1984.

Photo Peter Hanahoe.

Left
A remarkable view taken on June 16th 1973.
314 (40114) has derailed on the approach to Llandudno station whilst working the 10.40 from Manchester Victoria.
In this view, the passengers are seen being led from the stricken train towards the station platform, suitcases and domestic pets aplenty!
Photo Larry Davies.

Above
Immingham based 37283 at the head of 1E93, the 09.00 Llandudno to York on Saturday June 3rd 1978. This was the first class 37 hauled passenger working west of Rhyl, a notable sight indeed! Later refurbished and numbered 37895 she would eventually spend time in Spain working infrastructure traffic.

Right
An indication of the class 40 dominance on summer Saturdays in Llandudno! 40108/119/107 are seen waiting their return journeys in sidings just outside Llandudno station on July 24th 1979.
Photos Ron Watson-Jones.

British Rail (M) (1314)

CANMLWYDDIANT RHEILFFORDD DYFRYN CONWY

North Wales Railway Circle
Sunday July 22nd 1979

Llandudno — Blaenau Ffestiniog

CONWY VALLEY RAILWAY CENTENARY

2nd Class Adult   0026

For conditions see over

You may retain this ticket as a souvenir

Above
To celebrate the centenary of the Conwy Valley line the North Wales Railway Circle ran a special train from Crewe to Bangor, Llandudno and Blaenau Ffestiniog. Class 20's were chosen to work the train to commemorate the first Diesel to work along the Blaenau branch, see page 34. Here, the train hauled by 20153/165 is seen waiting departure from Llandudno with 40106, 40186 and 24081 also visible.
Photo Dave Plimmer.

Below
The section of line from Llandudno Junction to Llandudno was regularly used by class 40's. During summer months it was the ideal place to see members of the class from the likes of York, Healey Mills and Gateshead depots working trains laden with holidaymakers visiting the resort. In the view below, a more mundane working, 1J22, the 14.40 to Manchester Victoria is seen at Deganwy on July 10th 1983.
Photo Peter Hanahoe.

Above
40033 failed at Stalybridge whilst working 1M59, the 09.08 Scarborough to Llandudno on May 30th 1981. 25173 rescued the train but then failed itself at Warrington Bank Quay where 40140 was added to get the service through to its final destination!
In this view 40140 hauls dead 25173 and 40033 along the sea wall at Deganwy, running considerably late by now!
Photo Ron Watson-Jones.

Below
The first Diesel locomotive to visit the Blaenau branch was a class 20, and as early as February 19th 1961! D8036 (20036) was used to move a 123 Ton transformer from Hollinwood near Oldham to Blaenau Ffestiniog for use in a local Hydro Electric scheme. In this view the ensemble is seen pausing at Betws-y-Coed station during the journey.
Photo BR LMR.

Above
February 13th 1983 and 40060 sits at Dolgarrog with a train of spoil that is being unloaded as part of a scheme to strengthen the river bank at that location. Following withdrawal January 22nd 1985, this example would have a further lease of life in departmental service as 97405 up to March 1987.
Photo Dave Trains.

Below
40155 approaches Llanrwst station on June 12th 1983 with another train of spoil. It would run around the rake here before heading back to Dolgarrog for unloading, as with the train shown above. Interestingly, in common with 40060, 40155 would also run until "the end" in January 1985.
Photo Dave Trains.

Llandudno to Trawsfynydd

Right
Having reached Blaenau Ffestiniog on the Centenary special mentioned on page 33, the traincrew pause for photo's prior to the return journey.
July 22nd 1979.
Photo Dave Plimmer.

Below
Class 40's were often called on to provide additional power for charter trains over the difficult terrain to Blaenau Ffestiniog. In this view taken on September 11th 1983, 40001 pilots 47549 at Blaenau Ffestiniog on 1T08, a special working from London Euston.
Photo Peter Hanahoe.

Left
Up until the early 1980's the use of class 40's on the section of line from Blaenau to Trawsfynydd was rare if not unheard of. However, from May 1982, "Trip 47" from Llandudno Junction was booked for a 40. Amongst other things, this involved running all the way down to Trawsfynydd to pick up flasks from the local nuclear power station. In this view taken during 1982, Great Train Robbery celebrity 40126 is seen approaching what was once Cwm Teigl halt en route from Trawsfynydd conveying a single flask to Llandudno Junction. Here it would be combined with others from Valley for onward transit to the Sellafield reprocessing plant
Photo Merfyn Jones.

4.
Llandudno Junction to Bangor

Leaving "The Junction" the line passes the branch for Llandudno off to the right before heading through Stephenson's first tubular bridge opened in April 1848. It then curves right and left through Conwy and along Conwy Morfa before reaching the 718 yard Penmaenbach tunnel. An open stretch between the sea and steeply rising hills follows, running alongside the sea past Dwygyfylchi, an area popular with railway photographers alongside the A55 road. Penmaenmawr station and the quarry sidings on the right come next, a location that during the 1970's and 80's was a regular haunt for class 40's working a variety of ballast duties destined for various locations in the North West. There was even a reported class 50 visit here when 50021 was provided for a ballast working on June 7th 1974. On through Pen-y-Clip tunnel, into Llanfairfechan then along low ground through Aber, site of the first water troughs in the UK, laid by the LNWR in 1860 and still in use during the mid 1960's as can be seen on page 49! The line then crosses Ogwen Viaduct over the Afon Ogwen before passing through the 506 yard Llandygai tunnel and past the site of Penrhyn sidings which served Port Penrhyn via a short branch line until the early 1960's. Finally, on the left is the branch to Bethesda (closed October 1963), the junction being located just before the 913 yard long Bangor tunnel. Bangor station is situated between Bangor and Belmont tunnels with two through roads. A depot with a steam allocation is located on the left (closed 1964). The depot buildings remained intact following closure with a diesel shunter regularly out based here to service the goods yard adjacent to the shed. Signal boxes are located at either end of the station to control movements although No 1 box at the east end would disappear during 1969.

Above
July 9th 1966. D233 (40033) "Empress of England" approaches Llandudno Junction working the 09.55 Holyhead to Euston. This particular locomotive was to have a strong relationship with the area. Having been based at Holyhead for several months in 1959 for driver training she would go on to work the Prince of Wales Investiture Royal train with 216 in 1969, see page 57, before having to be transported by sea from Anglesey following the Britannia Bridge fire in May 1970, see page 89.
Photo Wyn Hobson.

Above
40069 shares part of Llandudno Junction carriage shed with 40022, 40003, 40170 and a solitary class 25 on February 2nd 1982. At this time the 40's were taking on more mundane duties during the rundown of the fleet including local Trip workings. It was therefore not uncommon to find several of them stabled at "The Junction" over a weekend.
Photo Ron Watson-Jones.

Left
Crewe North's D333 (40133) speeds through "The Junction" on June 27th 1964 heading an up Irish Mail working. A London Midland based locomotive throughout its life, the end of her career would come at Longsight depot on January 18th 1984 with cutting taking place at Donaster works within two months.
Photo Peter Owen.

Above
D231 (40031) "Sylvania" rounds the curve alongside Conwy station and Castle on an up passenger working in early 1963. The spur leading down to Conwy goods yard can be seen to the left alongside Conwy signal box.
Another casualty of the Britannia Bridge fire, 231 would leave Anglesey by road and boat in June 1970, see page 77!
Photo E N Kneale/S Morris collection.

Below
The Llandudno Junction/Holyhead Trip working 7T30 passes Conwy Morfa on the last leg of its journey behind 40135 on October 27th 1983. On this occasion the consist includes a bogie van full of Aluminium ingot from Anglesey Aluminium, empty 22T Castle Cement hoppers from Bangor and a solitary coal wagon from Valley goods yard.
Photo Peter Hanahoe.

Above
Longsight based 40055 rounds the curve at Conwy Morfa heading a rake of ex Iron Ore tipplers towards Penmaenmawr for loading. The date is May 28th 1982 and within six months this example would be withdrawn from service followed by cutting up at Doncaster works by May the following year.
Photo Peter Hanahoe.

Below
On the approach to Penmaenmawr at Dwygyfylchi. 40082 heads the 4D59 Trafford Park to Holyhead "Liner" during the evening of July 29th 1983.
Photo Peter Hanahoe.

Above
D297 (40097) is seen working "The Horse and Carriage" along the coast to the east of Penmaenmawr on May 2nd 1964. This was a midday ECS/Parcels working from Holyhead to Ordsall Lane Salford which collected surplus unbalanced stock from the likes of Bangor and Llandudno Junction en route resulting in a lengthy consist by the time it reached its destination!
Photo Peter Owen.

Below
40137 heads a lengthy train of Aluminium rolling ingot past Dwygyfylchi on the approach to Penmaenbach Tunnel on May 25th 1978. Trains of this type were rare, the majority of the output of Anglesey Aluminium by rail being in covered bogie Cargowagons.
Photo Ron Watson-Jones.

Left
November 16th 1961 and an early view of D320 (40120) heading for Holyhead on a stopping service from Crewe. The train is preparing to call at Penmaenmawr. The view from here has changed significantly during the last 50 years or so with the A55 dual carriageway now occupying the land under the photographer.
Photo Peter Owen.

Right
As mentioned previously, the sight of a class 37 in North Wales prior to the end of the 1980's was rare indeed. In this view, 37165 is seen passing Penmaenmawr heading for Holyhead working a special container train from the port of Felixstowe. She would return later that day on another special working, see page 77. This was the first visit for the class to Holyhead in daylight. Within a few years, class 37's would be a common feature in North Wales!
Date, April 8th 1983.
Photo Ron Watson-Jones.

Left
424 (50024) is seen with D209 (40009) passing Penmaenmawr on a running in turn from Crewe works during June 1971. The train is the mid afternoon departure from Bangor for Euston having worked down on 1D56, the 10.20 from the capital. For some reason the down headcode is displayed on the up train!
Photo Ron Watson-Jones.

Right

Crewe based 40194 is seen at Penmaenmawr "waiting the road" on an ECS working to Holyhead. Earlier that day she had failed at Sandycroft with low coolant, it seems as if it had been possible to top this up at some stage though. Interestingly, 40194 spent July to October 1977 on loan to the Western Region at Hereford for crew training purposes. Another of the final members of the class to be withdrawn from regular service, she would last until January 22nd 1985 with cutting at Doncaster works being completed within 5 weeks of this!
Date, March 31st 1983.
Photo Ron Watson-Jones.

Left

It is known that 40035 (Apapa) carried the last of the original class 40 nameplates in service, B bank side remaining in place until January 1975. However, what is not known is that she also "carried" another genuine plate, that from 40025 "Lusitania". In this view, 40035 is seen at Penmaenmawr yard with the plate fitted on B bank side following removal of the bodyside blanking bolts.
The date is March 28th 1983, and no, she did not run in traffic like this, the plate being removed prior to departure for St Helens!
So, one class 40 actually carried two different genuine nameplates!
Photos Ron Watson-Jones.

Right

A rare view of the evening TPO for Crewe, known locally as the "Mail Bach". 216 (40016) "Campania" is seen departing Penmaenmawr during May 1971, having worked a Royal train with 40025 a few weeks before. Normally starting at Holyhead, this service would have began at Bangor at 21.00 as it was during the time that the Britannia Bridge was closed following the fire of May 1970. On July 1st 1969, along with 233, 216 had worked the most significant "Royal" of all, see page 57.
Photo Ron Watson-Jones.

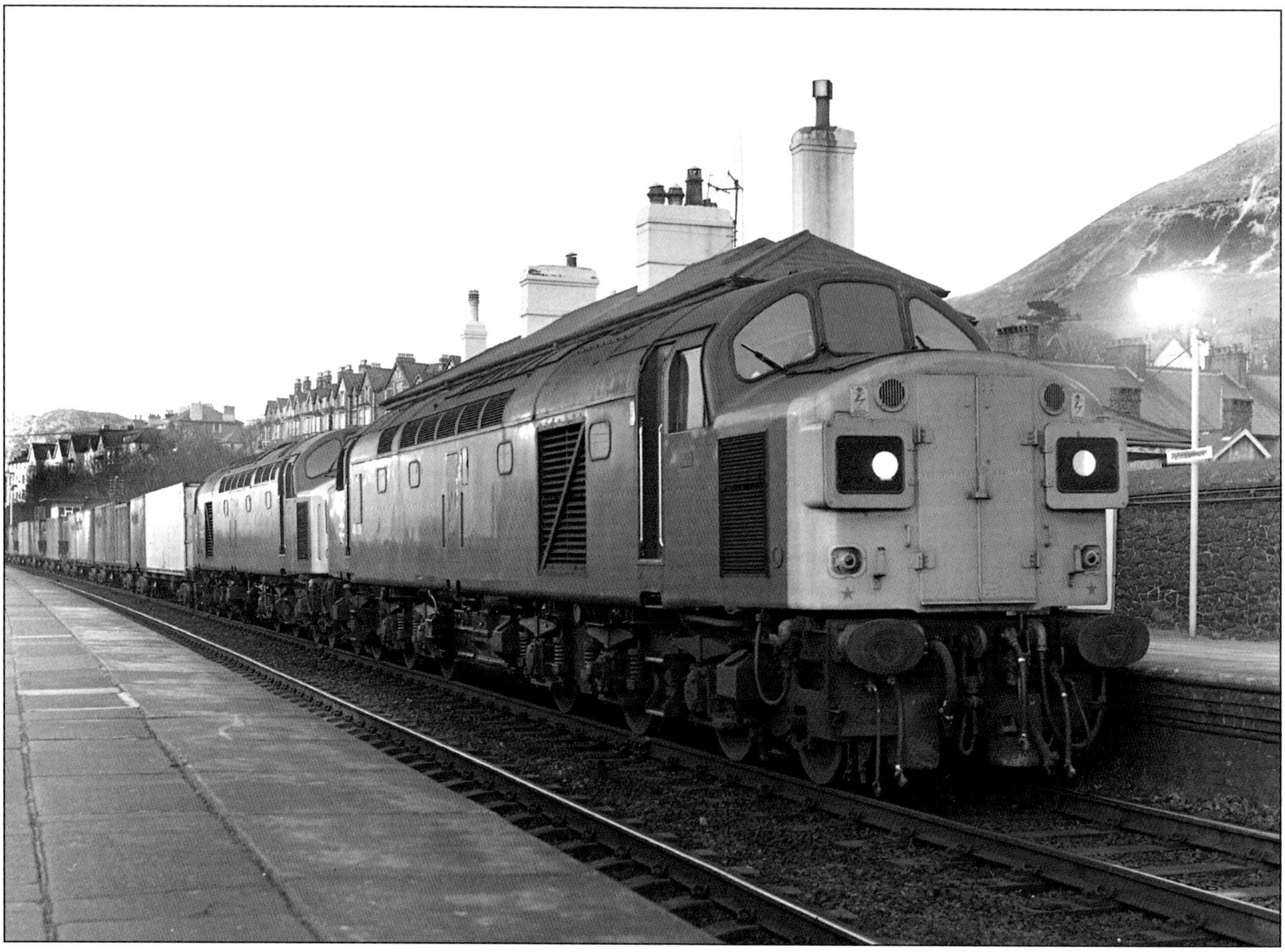

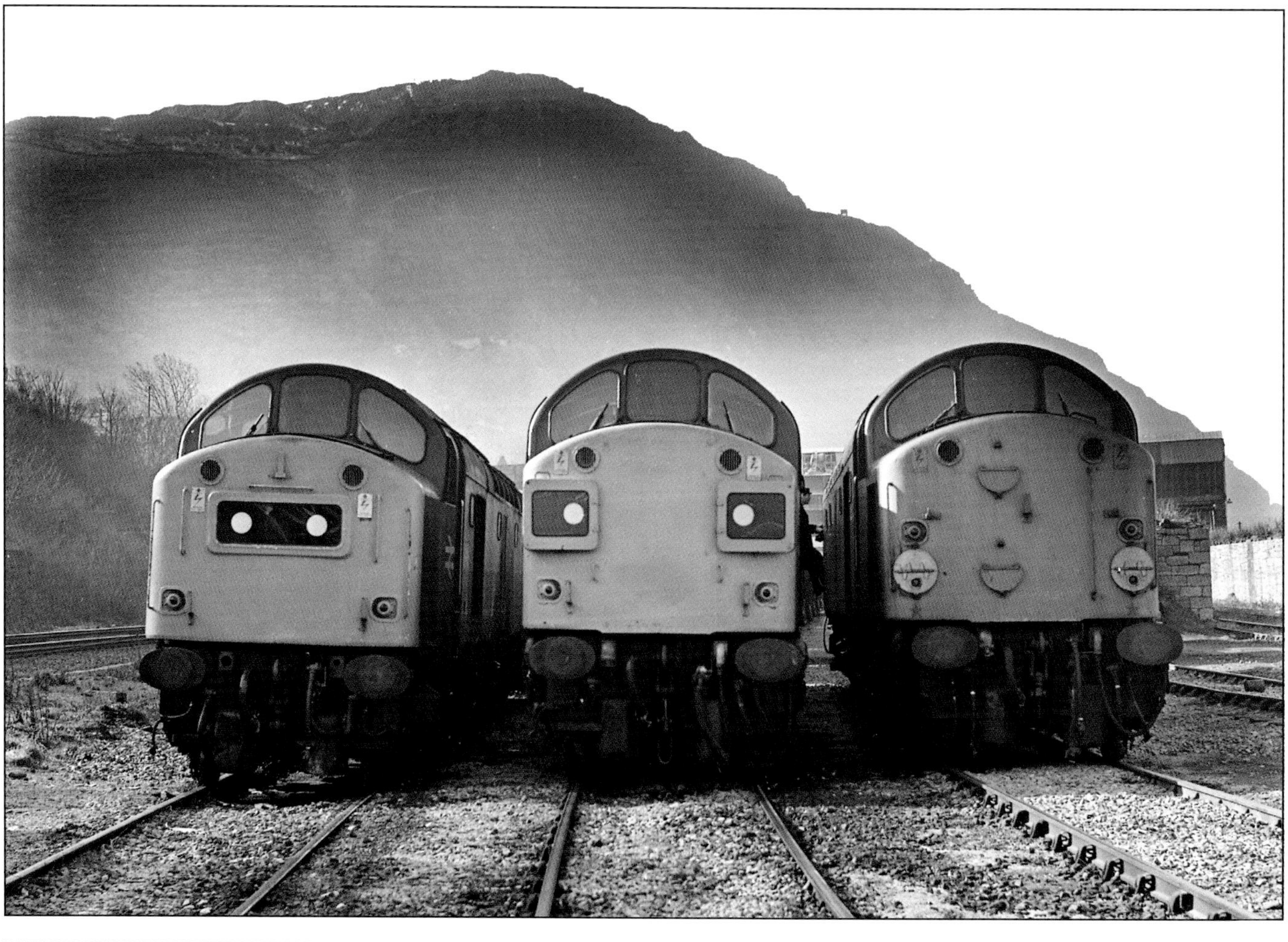

Above left
40129 and 40170 are held at Penmaenmawr station at dusk on a Holyhead bound Freightliner. April 14th 1981.

Below left
February 25th 1981 during the golden age of class 40 hauled stone trains out of Penmaenmawr! 40163, 144 and 086 line up to depart. **Photos Ron Watson-Jones.**

Above
40006 is seen loading for St Helens at Penmaenmawr quarry sidings. May 14th 1982.   **Photo Ron Watson-Jones.**

Below
40076 heads a Freightliner from Trafford Park through Penmaenmawr heading for Holyhead on June the 8th 1981. **Photo Peter Hanahoe.**

Above
A classic view of D268 (40068) heading a down evening stopping train west of Penmaenmawr station on April 6th 1964.

Left
D288 (40088) approaches Penmaenmawr on "The Horse and Carriage" on October 17th 1964. Note the cattle wagon next to the locomotive! The number 2 end cab, furthest from the camera, lives on in the ownership of The Class Forty Preservation Society, currently located at the Crewe Heritage Centre.   **Photos Peter Owen.**

Above right
Pen-y-Clip viaduct. 40104 is seen working 1D21, the 15.45 Manchester Victoria to Bangor during the evening of August 25th 1982. The lighting conditions to make the most of this location were only available for a short period each year, the results speak for themselves, a true North Wales Coast view!
Photo Ron Watson-Jones.

Below right
July 30th 1982. A superb evening view of Coast favourite 40033 approaching Llanfairfechan on a down Freightliner for Holyhead.
Photo Peter Hanahoe.

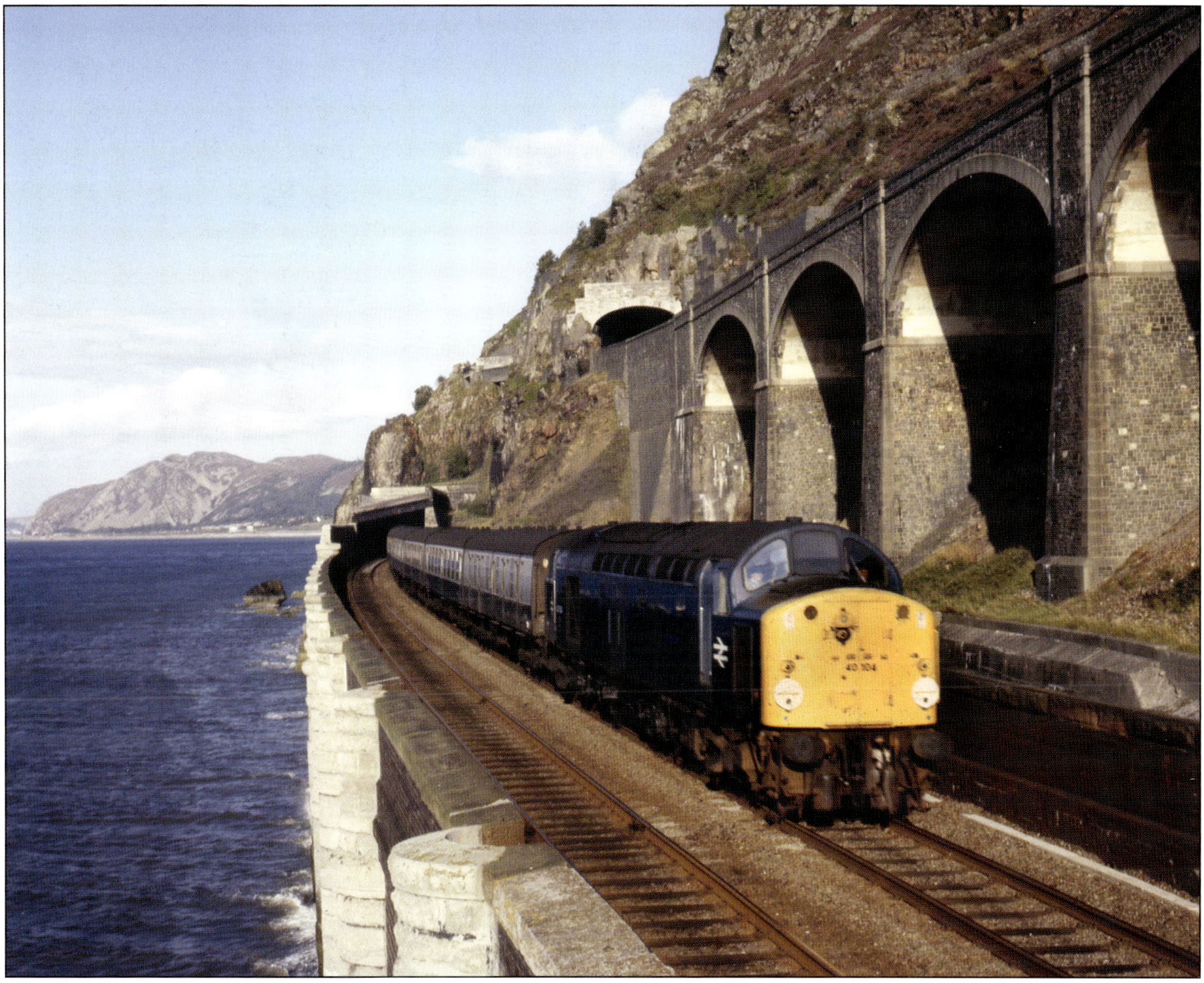

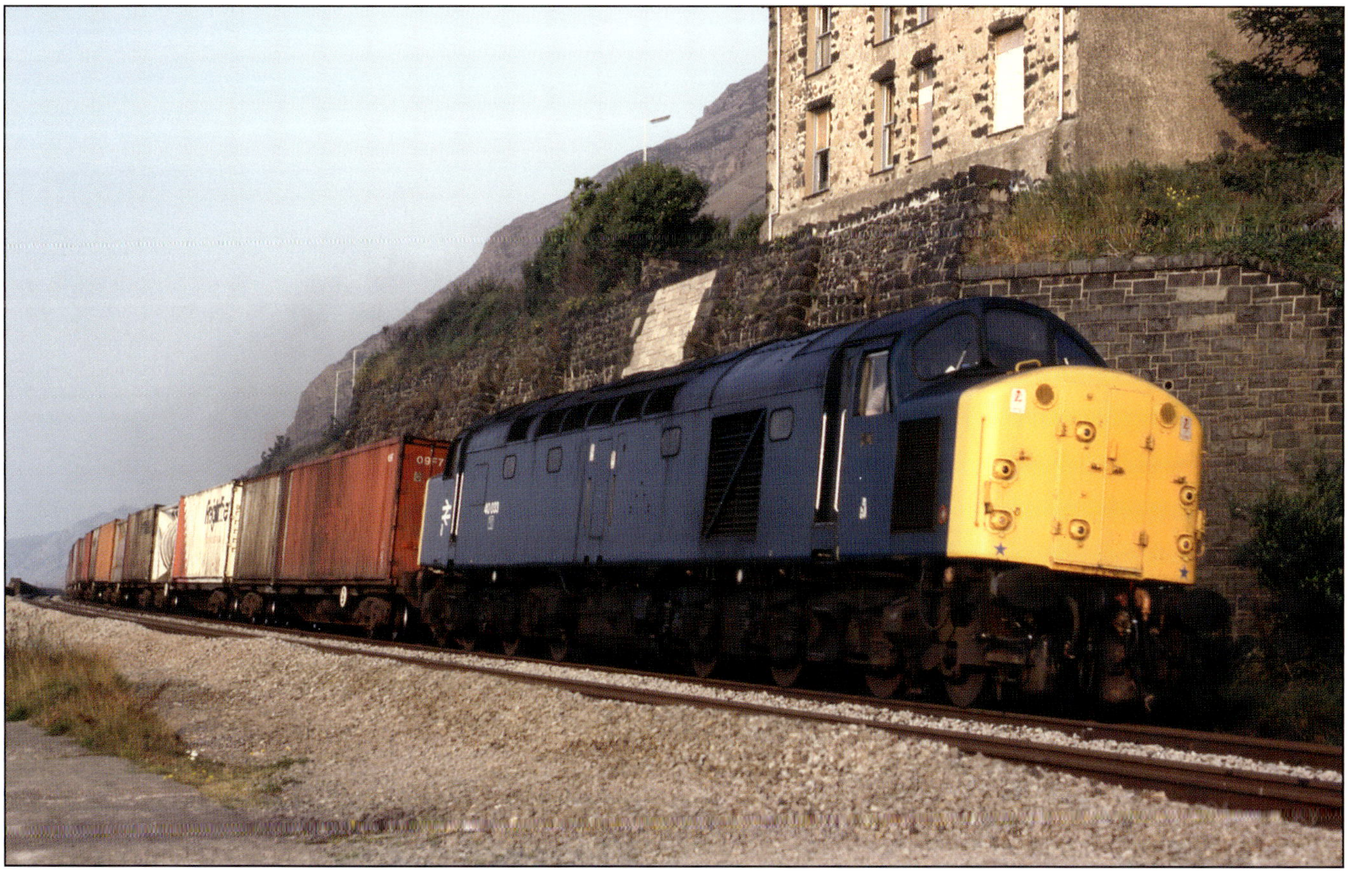

Llandudno Junction to Bangor

Above
June 5th 1981 and Healey Mills based 40085 has found its way onto a Manchester Victoria to Bangor diagram. Two return trips were performed. In this view she is seen at Pentr Du near Aber on 1D21, the 15.40 departure from Manchester. Return would be on the 1925 from Bangor. I wonder who the lucky lad in the cab is!
Photo Peter Hanahoe.

Below
40155 heads 4G58, the 14.40 Lawley Street to Holyhead "Liner" along the flat between Llanfairfechan and Bangor. Arrival was scheduled for 19.51 with the return working as 4G66 the next morning at 05.48.
May 24th 1983.
Photo Peter Hanahoe.

Above
Whilst class 40's were fitted with water scoops, operated by the Secondman to top up the train heating boiler, their use was rare. However, in this view taken on April 12th 1966, D232 (40032) "Empress of Canada" is captured taking water at Aber troughs whilst working the 12.55 Bangor to Euston.
Photo Wyn Hobson

Below
The Class Forty Preservation Society's very own 40135 is seen heading past Wig Crossing near Llanfairfechan whilst working the 4D59 Trafford Park to Holyhead container service. The date is July 15th 1983. The use of class 40's on these duties would soon start to reduce significantly.
Photo Peter Hanahoe.

Above
D307 (40107) on the last few miles to Bangor heading a down stopping service on July 19th 1969. Class 47's had now started to take over a number of the duties previously handled by class 40's and appearances on secondary duties such as this were becoming more common towards the end of the 1960's.
Photo Barry Wynne.

Above
Delivered new to Haymarket in November 1961, 40166 was one of the first of the class to be transferred south, the move coming to Longsight as early as May 1978.
In this view taken on June 9th 1981, she is seen at "Gypsy Corner" on the outskirts of Bangor heading the 5H09 empty vans from Bangor to Manchester Red Bank.
Photo Peter Hanahoe.

Left
D249 (40049) heads a down Irish Mail working at Talybont on the approach to Bangor during August 1969.
Allocated to the "Preston Division" at the time she would move to York depot in 1971 and remain an Eastern Region loco until transfer to Longsight to see out the final six months before withdrawal in January 1983. **Photo Barry Wynne.**

Above
The first class 20 working west of Llandudno Junction took place on July 22nd 1979 with 20153-20165 working the North Wales Railway Circle Conwy Valley Centenary special from Crewe, see also page 33. In this view they are seen on 1L03, the return from Bangor near Talybont. Next stop Llandudno.
Photo Dave Trains.

Below
The Associated Octel plant at Amlwch received regular loads of sulphur by rail from Mostyn Docks conveyed in covered vacuum braked HJV/HKV wagons. One such working passes the site of what was Penrhyn sidings near Bangor on October 26th 1983 behind 40126. The final train ran on May 17th 1989.
Photo Peter Hanahoe.

Above
40027 "Parthia" heads the 1J66
Bangor to Manchester out of
Bangor tunnel on February 14th
1981. The area to the right, now
overgrown, was once home to
Penrhyn sidings that served Port
Penrhyn near Bangor until the
early 1960's.
Photo Peter Hanahoe.

Right
Double headed class 40's. D210
(40010) "Empress of Britain"
exits Bangor tunnel with 244
(40044) working an up relief to
The Irish Mail on July 19th 1969.
Until closure in 1963, the branch
to Bethesda had diverged to the
left of the picture although it is
has long since been lifted.
As can be seen, D210's A bank
nameplate has already been
removed.
Photo Barry Wynne.

Above
A classic early view of a class 40 in action! Carlisle Upperby allocated D236 (40036) leaves Bangor heading the 12.50 Holyhead to Euston on April 13th 1963.
Photo Barry Wynne.

Below
D333 (40133) emerges from Bangor tunnel on 1D16, the 09.20 Crewe to Holyhead during the summer of 1963. This particular example would remain based on the "LM" throughout her life of just under 23 years.
Photo Barry Wynne.

Above
D226 (40026) storms through the centre road at Bangor during The summer of 1963 on an up boat train. The shed on the left would close on June 12th 1965.
Photo E N Kneale/S Morris collection.

Below
D330 (40130) has just arrived at Bangor on a van train. The loco is in excellent external condition with signs of it having recently worked a Royal train. June 12th 1968.
Photo Barry Wynne.

Left
Up until the mid 1970's, class 50's were relatively frequent visitors to Bangor on running in turns from Crewe works. In this view an unidentified member of the class is seen about to depart Bangor on what is probably the 15.10 Euston working with the booked class 47 as insurance.
Photo The late D Bate.

Right
20153/20165 are about to depart Bangor on 1L03 to Llandudno and Blaenau Ffestiniog on July 22nd 1979. At this time this was the furthest along the North Wales Coast route that class 20's had operated.
**Photo
Dave Plimmer.**

Left
40004 sits in Bangor station on top of 4J09, the 08.25 empty vans for Manchester Red Bank. The date is July 30th 1983 and within a few years newspaper traffic would be consigned to the history books following transfer to road haulage.
Note the Wessex helicopter from RAF Valley hovering in the background!
Photo Peter Hanahoe.

Above

The first class 37 hauled passenger working west of Llandudno took place on May 6th 1983. 37173 had worked an additional container train into Holyhead that afternoon, this in itself a notable event. Whilst working back light engine, and after a layover in Bangor due to the crew running out of hours, she was called upon to work the 19.25 Bangor to Manchester due to the failure of 47481. In this view the train is seen running into Bangor station to take up the working.
Photo Peter Hanahoe.

Below

By the early 1980's, class 45's started to appear in North Wales with increasing frequency. In this view taken on June 23rd 1983, 45069 having failed in Bangor station whilst waiting to work 1J31, the 19.30 to Manchester Victoria, has been rescued by 40080. The pair are seen about to depart the station, the first such combination to be seen in the area. This was repeated a few weeks later on July 18th 1983 with 40197 and a failed 45023 on IE53, the 13.24 Llandudno to Scarborough, from Llandudno Junction to York .   **Photo Dave Trains.**

5.
Caernarfon branch

The eight mile branch for Caernarfon left the mainline at Menai Bridge. It was basically the remains of the line that ran through to the Cambrian line at Afon Wen which was closed past Caernarfon in December 1964. Class 40's were employed relatively frequently on the route, mainly on summer dated holiday trains from the Manchester and Liverpool areas, many of which conveyed passengers for the Butlins camp at Pwllheli. From 1964 onwards they were conveyed the remaining distance by bus! A number of class 40 hauled Royal Trains traversed the line, the most notable being on July 1st 1969 in association with the Prince of Wales Investiture, see below.

The line was closed to freight in August 1969 followed by complete closure on January 5th 1970. However, following the disastrous fire within the Britannia Bridge on May 23rd of the same year, the line was reopened to freight between June 15th 1970 and the 5th of February 1972 during which a regular Freightliner working was implemented for unloading at Caernarfon to allow final transport of the containers to Holyhead by road. Class 40's were rarely provided for these or the other occasional freight workings seen during this temporary reprieve for the line.

Above
The most significant class 40 passenger working in North Wales took place on July 1st 1969 when 233 (40033) "Empress of England" and 216 (40016) "Campania" worked the Prince of Wales Investiture Royal Train throughout between Euston and Caernarfon. In this view the inbound working is seen approaching a temporary platform at Griffiths Crossing just outside Caernarfon at 2pm having spent the previous night stabled in Menai Bridge yard. In the foreground the Household Cavalry is seen waiting to act as two separate escorts to Caernarfon Castle, one for the Prince and one as a Sovereign escort to the Queen. Interestingly the horses and men concerned had been transported from London to Bangor by train hauled by class 47 number 1719 (47811) before being ridden to Caernarfon prior to the event. This was the last occasion that the Household Cavalry was transported by rail.
On the day of the Investiture, class 47 locomotives 1718 (47539) in tandem with 1692 (47104) worked another service in from Crewe along with 1723 (47540) and 1719 (47811) taking over from electric traction on two other departures from Euston. Also, 1591 (47557), 1592 (47544) and 1593 (47467) covered workings from Cardiff. Last but not least, class 40's 207 (40007) and 242 (40042) were also used as Royal Train pilot locomotives during the proceedings!
Photo E N Kneale/S Morris collection.

Above
During the summer of 1963, D308 (40108) was used on several Royal Train workings. In this view she can be seen climbing up the Caernarfon branch from Menai Bridge station heading for Caernarfon on one such duty. After such an illustrious start to her career she would become an early withdrawal victim, the end coming in August 1980.
Photo E N Kneale/S Morris collection.

Below
The summer of 1969. 256 (40056) is seen waiting to leave Caernarfon on 1F03, the summer Saturday 13.38 departure for Warrington. By now this was the only loco hauled service along the branch to Caernarfon and it was to be the last summer of any passenger workings to the town with closure coming the following January.
Photo The late Bill Rear.

Above

As mentioned in the introduction to this chapter, the Caernarfon branch reopened to freight between June 1970 and February 1972 as a result of the Britannia Bridge fire. One of the regular services to use the line was a daily Freightliner service which was unloaded at Caernarfon for onward transport by road to Holyhead port. Class 47's were almost always used for this duty but on September 1st 1970 D370 (40170) was provided, a rare occurrence indeed. In this view she can be seen near Port Dinorwic about three miles from Menai Bridge on the 4G50 afternoon return working to Birmingham Lawley Street
Photo Wyn Hobson.

Below

Token exchange at Menai Bridge. The summer of 1967 and D378 (40178) runs off the Caernarfon branch through the station, closed the previous year, on the 15.00 Caernarfon to Liverpool. Once again, this was a summer Saturday dated service running June 17th to September 2nd this particular year. The main customers were holiday makers for Butlins in Pwllheli. They would be met by road coaches at Caernarfon station for the remaining twenty mile journey to the camp. This was the final year of loco haulage for this service, being replaced by a DMU in 1968.
Photo E N Kneale/S Morris collection.

6.
Bangor to Holyhead

On departing Bangor the line immediately enters the 648 yard Belmont Tunnel before winding its way alongside the Menai Strait with views of Telford's suspension bridge to the right. Next comes Menai Bridge station (closed February 1966) and yard, with the branch to Caernarfon heading off up an incline to the left. Then it is onto Stephenson's Britannia Bridge linking the mainland to Anglesey, a tubular structure as at Conwy but this time 504 yards long and over 100 feet above water level! A huge fire which started on May 23rd 1970 resulted in the closure of the bridge so severing the rail link to Anglesey until reopening in a modified form, minus the tubes, on January 30th 1972. A road deck was then added, opening in July 1980.

On leaving the bridge the line curves to the left and on through "Llanfair PG", for the full version see page 72! Next comes Gaerwen, the station would close in December 1964 but the branch to Amlwch off to the right remained open throughout the period covered by this volume, see page 80. West of Gaerwen the line descends the 1 in 97/102 Llangaffo Bank to sea-level and Malltraeth Marsh. Over Bodorgan viaduct then a 1 in 98 climb through two tunnels on the approach to Bodorgan station before heading through Ty Croes and Rhosneigr, with views of RAF Valley on the left. Soon we approach Valley, with sidings to the right for general use and from the early 1970's onwards, a loading point for nuclear flasks from the nearby Wylfa power station, often class 40 hauled. It was also the place where seven class 40's would have their bogies removed prior to shipping to the mainland following the Britannia Bridge fire, see page 76. The line then runs onto the Stanley Embankment, a causeway linking Anglesey with Holy Island before passing the RTZ Anglesey Aluminium smelter, opened in 1970 and served by numerous class 40 and even two class 37 hauled freights during the period covered by this volume. Then a drop down a 1 in 135 gradient past Ty Mawr farm on the left and then the water tower on the right follows before the line runs under what was locally known as "Canada Gardens" bridge to pass between Holyhead depot on the right and cattle/goods yard on the left. We then reach the end of the line at Holyhead station, just over 84 miles from Chester.

Above
A classic view of the west end of Bangor station during the summer of 1963. Crewe North allocated D319 (40119) is about to enter Belmont tunnel heading a down passenger working for Holyhead whilst Bangor based Black Five 45345 comes off the shed to replace the incoming traction on 1D26, a summer Saturday dated 09.05 Liverpool Lime Street to Penychain service. By the time this image was recorded, class 40's had been covering passenger services in North Wales for over three years and were increasingly replacing steam traction, although it would take a further four years for this transition to be complete. D319 would remain a "London Midland" loco throughout it's career being withdrawn in December 1980 after a relatively short life of under 20 years. Cutting up came at Swindon works in October 1982.
Photo E N Kneale/S Morris collection.

Above

A classic shot of D309 (40109) storming through Bangor on an up Irish Mail working during the summer of 1963. Based at Edge Hill at the time, 40109 would, as with 40119 on the opposite page, have a relatively short working life of under twenty years, withdrawal coming in November 1980 from Carlisle Kingmoor. **Photo E N Kneale/S Morris collection.**

Below

D231 (40031) "Sylvania" calls at Bangor on an up service for Manchester in the winter of 1965. The locomotive still carries green livery but signs of the new corporate blue era are seen in the rake of coaches behind.

Photo E N Kneale/S Morris collection.

Above
Transition period at Bangor. D369 (40169) races through the station on a Holyhead to Mold Junction merchandise service whilst a grubby 44685 waits to depart light to Holyhead shed. It is August 1st 1966, just under 12 months before the final steam working in North Wales.
Photo Barry Wynne.

Below
A fine study of the west end of Bangor station looking east right through Bangor tunnel. An early recipient of corporate blue livery was D206 (40006). In this view she is seen waiting to depart Bangor on the 13.50 stopping train to Holyhead on October 4th 1969. A DMU for Caernarfon is seen in number 1 bay platform. **Photo Barry Wynne.**

Above
The Class Forty Preservation Society's 40145 calls at Bangor at the head of the 08.55 Euston to Holyhead on August 22nd 1982. She would later return on 1A47, the 18.07 Holyhead to Euston as far as Crewe.
Photo Peter Hanahoe.

Below
The same day as the above image was recorded. This time it is Longsight based 40184 working 1J50, the 14.44 Holyhead to Manchester having worked down on the 12.40 Llandudno Junction to Holyhead earlier that day.
Photo Peter Hanahoe.

Above
Bangor station during the summer of 1982. 40093 and 40121 are seen engaged in work associated with track replacement in the area. By now, 093 was a Springs Branch based locomotive and would have been a relatively frequent visitor to the area. However, 40121 was a true Eastern Region freight example based at Healey Mills, for a few more months at least, with a final allocation to Longsight taking place in October.
Photo Peter Hanahoe.

Below
D370 (40170) is seen between the Belmont tunnel and Menai Bridge station working the 06.00 Crewe to Bangor parcels, extended to Holyhead on this particular day. The date is April 15th 1967 and with steam nearing its end in North Wales class 40's were now the main choice of motive power for these workings as well as the passenger duties that they had started to take over some seven years earlier.
Photo Wyn Hobson.

Above
An unidentified class 40 heads a down passenger service past Menai Bridge yard in the summer of 1964. The Caernarfon branch heads off at right of this location passing under another of the arches of the bridge and alongside the photographer.
Photo E N Kneale/S Morris collection.

Below
April 1965. D308 (40108) passes through Menai Bridge station on an up Manchester working during the spring of 1965. The station itself would be closed the following February.
Photo E N Kneale/S Morris collection.

Above
D214 (40014) "Antonia" and D225 (40025) "Lusitania" pass Menai Bridge signal box on an up working during early 1964. Double headed class 40's were not common and to get two "namers" on the same train was certainly a bonus!

Right
North Wales regular D233 (40033) speeds through the now closed Menai Bridge station during the summer of 1966 on a stopping service for Crewe.

Photos E N Kneale/S Morris collection.

Above
Following the Britannia Bridge fire of May 23rd 1970, a temporary loading facility for cattle trains was introduced on the up platform of the disused Menai Bridge station to allow the continued running of the service. Imported cattle from Ireland were transported by road from Holyhead to the station for loading onto the daily service to York Holgate Dock, where they would be handed over to local farmers for fattening. Commencing in November 1970, the facility was used until the bridge reopened in January 1972 during which time over 105,000 cattle were loaded onto trains bound for Yorkshire!
In this view, 391 (40191) waits to depart Menai Bridge on 6E66 the 17.43 departure on March 13th 1971. The final cattle train would leave Holyhead behind a pair of class 24's on November 30th 1975 bringing the carriage of livestock by rail to an end.
Photo E N Kneale/S Morris collection.

Right
D319 (40119) passes a very impressive array of signalling on the approach to Menai Bridge whilst heading a down passenger working during the summer of 1964 .
Photo E N Kneale/ S Morris collection.

Above
40035 passes the site of the disused Menai Bridge yard at the head of 4D58, the 14.40 Lawley Street to Holyhead "Liner" during the evening of May 9th 1983.
Photo Dave Trains.

Below
No book of this nature would be complete without this view! An unidentified class 40 is seen working an up Irish Mail off Britannia Bridge during March 1963.
Photo E N Kneale/S Morris collection.

Above

A view which demonstrates the changes made to the Britannia Bridge and its surroundings following rebuilding after the fire. The trademark tubes have gone leaving the supporting pillars onto which a road deck has been added. The lions guarding the start of the bridge remain in place and act as a handy reference point for comparison to the image on the previous page. The track is now singled. 40143 curves to the left off the bridge on a Holyhead to Manchester service in the summer of 1983.

Left

Mid rebuild! Having been re opened on January 30th 1972, work on Britannia Bridge progressed for a number of years. In this view the removal of the tubular section on the up line is still underway, all traffic now using the down line which has had the fire damaged tube removed. The road deck would not be added for several years to come, finally being opened in May 1980.

In this view taken on April 9th 1974, 310 (40110) crosses the bridge on a Trafford Park bound Freightliner.

Photos E N Kneale/S Morris collection.

Above

One of seven class 40's marooned on Anglesey following the Britannia Bridge fire was D219 (40019) "Caronia". They were shipped off the island by the middle of June 1970, some 3 weeks after the fire. To cater for passenger traffic, a temporary station platform was built at Llanfair PG and used between May 29th 1970 and January 31st 1972. The original station had been a victim of Dr Beeching and closed in 1966, although it was to fully re-open in May 1973. In this view, taken just after the temporary station had opened, D219 is seen stabled alongside Llanfair PG signal box. At this time, several passenger services from Holyhead to Llanfair PG were worked by class 40's and four MK1 coaches and this is the reason for D219 being parked here. Following the repatriation of the 40's, these services were worked by class 24's 5043 or 5083, or a two car DMU which remained on the island throughout the bridge closure.

Photo Barry Wynne.

Right

Llanfair PG. 212 (40012) "Aureol" is seen at the head of an up "Liner" on the 28th October 1973. This was only a few months following the full re-opening of the station, the wooden platform built on the up side for use during the Bridge closure period having been replaced by permanent structures serving both lines. Following withdrawal in February 1985, 40012 spent a period in departmental service as 97407 before entering preservation at the Midland Railway Centre Butterley in 1989.

Photo Ian Langhorn.
www.the-transport-photo-interchange.co.uk

Above
40181 is seen during track replacement work on the approach to Llanfair PG during April 3rd 1983.
Photo Peter Hanahoe.

Below
Ex works 40035 "Apapa" approaches Llanfair PG working wrong line during Sunday engineering works. The train is the Sundays Only 1D54, 08.35 Euston to Holyhead.
Photo Dave Trains.

Above
Llanfairpwllgwyngyllgogerychwyrndrobwllllantysiliogogogoch!
The longest station name in the UK, shortened to Llanfair PG for
obvious reasons! Ex works 40099 passes through heading 1A27,
the 13.09 Holyhead to Euston on August 24th 1980.
Photo Dave Trains.

Below
40158 heads for Holyhead port on the 4D59 Freightliner
from Trafford Park during the evening of June 27th 1983.
The location is Llanddaniel near to Gaerwen and the branch
to Amlwch. Six months later she would be withdrawn from
Kingmoor depot. **Photo Peter Hanahoe.**

Above
D382 (40182) thunders across Anglesey between Gaerwen and Llanfair PG on the 13.25 Holyhead to Euston. Summer 1963.
Photo E N Kneale/S Morris collection.

Below
A superb, if not unique image recorded between the two tunnels at Bodorgan, taken by prior arrangement! 40106 has just passed through Bodorgan station at the brow of the hill and heads for Manchester on the 15.17 from Holyhead. September 1st 1982.
Photo Ron Watson-Jones.

Above
The "Horse and Carriage", see page 41 for a full description, is seen at Ty Croes behind D343 (40143) during July 1964. Stops at Bangor and Llandudno Junction to add more stock would be ahead and it is already loaded to 15 vehicles leaving Holyhead!
Photo Barry Wynne.

Below
40082 opens up on the last leg of her journey to Holyhead with a Freightliner at Rhosneigr on July 27th 1983. These services would continue for a further eight years, the final train leaving the port behind 47301 on March 18th 1991.
Photo Peter Hanahoe.

Above
40157 is seen near RAF Valley heading 1D38, the 11.55 Manchester to Holyhead on June 13th 1982. Just over 12 months later she would suffer and engine room fire whilst heading the Stirling to Euston Motorail service bringing her career to an abrupt end!
Photo Peter Hanahoe.

Left
Having moved to Carlisle Kingmoor after over 20 years based at Haymarket, 40060 became a frequent visitor to North Wales during the last 5 years of her career and when in departmental service as 97405. In this view she is seen on an up Freightliner through Valley on April 23rd 1982.
Photo Garnedd Jones.

Right
Another long term Haymarket class 40 transferred south following the end of regular duties for them north of the border was 40065. However, in this case the loco concerned would only last 9 months before withdrawal, the end coming at Kingmoor depot as early as November 1981. There then followed a period in store at Reddish depot before a trip across to Crewe works in August 1982. Cutting was not completed until March 1985.
Here, 40065 approaches Valley working the 09.10 Holyhead to Manchester Victoria on August 30th 1981, having worked down with 40036 the day before, see page 6.
Photo Pat Webb.

Above
An early view of a brand new D331 (40131) heading an up service through Valley in March 1961. Note the particularly short consist considering the "Euston" headcode.
Photo rail-online.co.uk.

Below
Coast favourite 233 is seen at Valley yard in the process of having her bogies removed to allow road transfer to Holyhead and shipping to Barrow. June 13th 1970. Also see page 89.
Photo Ron Watson-Jones.

Right
40155 departs Valley on 6P40, the 15.45 CEGB Valley to Sellafield flask train. The flask wagons are of the older XKB "flatrol" design and ex RBX Ferrywagons are included as barrier vehicles.
The date is May 11th 1983. Who would have thought that over 18 years later, English Electric traction would still be involved in these workings, more of this in volume two!
Photo Dave Trains.

Left
No apologies for another view of 37165, see page 42, it was after all an unusual sight! Here she can be seen on the approach to Valley with the up working on April 8th 1983 having spent less than an hour in the port after arriving on a down "Liner" from Felixstowe.
Photo Colin Webb.

Below
June 1970. 231 (40031) "Sylvania" has lost its bogies at Valley and is in the process of being transferred to Holyhead for shipping to the mainland a few weeks after the Britannia Bridge fire. The bogies were towed down to the port by a class 24.
Photo Pat Webb.

Above
40063 passes Valley coal yard on a wintery 20th February 1982 en route Holyhead. It is working the 8T92 trip from Llandudno Junction. Most of the load comprises empty Cargowagons destined for Anglesey Aluminium. These will be deposited, and any loaded ones collected, on the return.
Photo Dave Trains.

Below
40033 on the final approach to Holyhead working 4M50, the 01.35 Freightliner from Ripple Lane which was due to arrive at the port at 10.24. Date, December 16th 1983.
Photo Steve Morris.

Above right
The 13.05 Holyhead to Euston passes the water tower on the climb out of Holyhead behind 40029 "Saxonia" on June 27th 1981. She would later return on the 17.25 from Crewe.

Below right
The first and last working of a class 40 hauled MK3 rake to Holyhead occurred on September 2nd 1983 when 40195 worked in on a 15.05 relief from Crewe. She immediately ran around the stock and headed back ECS to Edge Hill, as seen in this image taken just outside the town.
Photos Steve Morris.

7.
Amlwch branch

Leaving the mainline at Gaerwen, the branch to Amlwch was opened fully in 1867. During the period covered by this volume it was used by steam and DMU operated passenger traffic until December 1964 but the main involvement of English Electric traction came from the 1970's onwards with numerous class 40 hauled freight services traversing the line. In the main these involved workings to and from the Associated Octel chemical plant at Amlwch. Trainloads of sulphur were transported there from Mostyn Dock. In the other direction consignments of chlorine and ethylene dybromide were despatched from Amlwch to Ellesmere Port and anti-knock compound to a number of UK and European refineries, altogether this amounted to a total of approximately 70,000 tonnes per annum. In addition, during the mid 1970's class 40's made occasional visits to a spur off the branch at Rhosgoch to deliver pipes for a pipeline from the Shell Oil storage tanks on the site to their Stanlow refinery, see page 82. Also, from the early 1980's they started to turn up on Trip workings from Llandudno Junction. Finally, during the 1980's a number of class 40 hauled charter trains visited the line. The first of these, as shown on pages 82 and 84, was the "Amlwch Pioneer" top and tailed by 40058 and 40034 in May 1983.

Above
July 20th 1983. 40172 is seen heading 7D05 the Amlwch to Llandudno Junction tanks at "The Dingle" Llangefni. The final destination for the load from Associated Octel would be Ellesmere Port. The post for the former Llangefni up distant signal is seen in the foreground. The last working of this service took place behind 31126 on February 10th 1994 although its frequency had been much reduced since September of the previous year. Closed for over 17 years there are rumours circulating about a possible re opening of the line to cater for tourists and possibly to transport materials needed for the potential Wylfa B nuclear power station project. As for 40172, she would remain in traffic for only a further seven weeks from this date before being withdrawn from service at Crewe Diesel depot.
Photo Peter Hanahoe.

Above
40172 arrives at the exchange sidings at Amlwch with the daily 7D04 working from Llandudno Junction during the summer of 1983. The wagons would soon be collected by onc of the resident industrial shunters and transferred up the short spur to the Associated Octel facility.
Photo Peter Hanahoe.

Below
The second passenger charter to traverse the Amlwch branch during 1983 was the "Menai Marauder" run by F&W tours from Plymouth on July 3rd. 40093 and 40028 were provided. In this view it is seen at the site of the disused Rhosgoch Tank Farm sidings on the return working heading for Gaerwen with 40093 up front . **Photo Dave Trains.**

Amlwch branch

Left and below
Shell Oil constructed a Tank Farm south of Amlwch at Rhosgoch. Crude oil was to be pumped from offshore tankers to the storage tanks before being piped to Shell's Stanlow refinery. Several trains associated with the laying of the pipeline to Stanlow ran to a siding built on the site during the mid 1970's. In this view, 40113 is seen arriving with a trainload of pipes and then on the siding itself after depositing the wagons concerned. The line on towards Amlwch can be seen ahead. She would then return with a trainload of empties from the previous delivery. These trains did not run very often and the view of a 40 actually on the siding itself is particularly rare. The whole concept was flawed and the site was only used for a short period before being closed down.
Photo E N Kneale/S Morris collection.

Below
The first class 40 hauled passenger train on the Amlwch branch ran as the "Amlwch Pioneer" from Euston on May 14th 1983. Top and tailed by 40058 and 40034 it is seen at Cefni Reservoir with "058" leading on the outbound working.
There is currently talk of the Amlwch branch reopening in conjunction with the building of Wylfa B Nuclear power station, time will tell if this comes to anything!
Photo E N Kneale/S Morris collection.

Above
40097 is seen at Llanerchymedd heading for Warrington Arpley with 7F12, the 14.54 departure from Amlwch on October 17th 1980. By now, class 40's were taking over more and more of the local freight duties in North Wales.
Photo Dave Trains.

Below
Another view of the "Menai Marauder" tour, see page 81, this time at Llangefni. 40028 heads the outbound train with 40093 seen here at the rear. A third class 40 hauled tour would cover the route in 1983, this time 40122 top and tailed with 47537 with the "Britannia Belle" on December 10th.
Photo Peter Hanahoe.

Above
Another view of the "Amlwch Pioneer" heading for Amlwch behind 40058 with 40034 hidden out of view as the train passes slowly through Llangefni. This was the first passenger train to run to Amlwch since closure to this traffic in 1964, and certainly the first class 40 hauled passenger on the branch from Gaerwen.
As mentioned earlier, two other "specials" would follow before the end of 1983, both featuring class 40 haulage.
Photo Dave Trains.

Below
40152 "gets the road" to join the mainline at Gaerwen on a soggy September 8th 1983 working 7D05, the return daily service from Amlwch to Llandudno Junction .
This particular example would work the last timetabled class 40 hauled passenger train in North Wales by heading 1E93, the 17.30 Bangor to York on January 17th 1985 following failure of the booked class 47. Lack of train heat resulted in the service being terminated at Chester and it going forward ECS to York.
Photo Peter Hanahoe.

8.
Holyhead

The end of the line! Holyhead first played host to English Electric traction in 1959, see page 86. As with the other sections of this book, class 40's were the most regular "EE" product to make it as far as Holyhead. The class started regular association with the town on April 25th 1960 following dieselisation of "The Irish Mail" and "Emerald Isle Express" to and from London Euston which they worked throughout. During the 1960's they were then used in increasing numbers covering all manner of passenger workings to the port as well as longer distance freight duties such as those covering movements of containers and cattle. From 1970 it included Freightliner trains as well as LPG and petroleum coke workings for the nearby Aluminium smelter and by the early 80's local trip workings as well. Class 47's started to make inroads into their territory from the late 60's onwards but the class were regular visitors to Holyhead throughout the period covered by this volume. For example, on a typical Sunday in the mid 1970's it was not unusual to find up to ten members of the class stabled on Holyhead shed!

Whilst they had been working as far as Llandudno and Bangor for several years, sometimes on test following attention at Crewe works, class 50's did not make it all the way through to Holyhead until the mid 1970's. A number of appearances were made on the 19.15 down Euston and 00.55 return as well as the 4D62 Freightliner from Willesden during 1975/76, which they worked from Crewe. There was also the odd appearance on ECS workings or arriving light engine to head the lunchtime summer boat train as far as Crewe. The final working during this period involved 50046 on the 19.15/00.55 duty over the night of 11/12th June 1976.

Class 37's made very few visits to the port up to the end of 1983, strange when you consider how common they would become in later years! Apart from two reported visits on the Anglesey Aluminium "coke" and the two special container train workings covered earlier in the book, that was it.

Above
An image highlighting the fact that EE traction ruled in North Wales! Taken just prior to the closure of Holyhead shed to steam in December 1966, four class 40's are seen on the depot waiting their next duty. There is not a steam locomotive in sight but the depot still has the feel of the former choice of motive power about it.
London Midland based D377 (40177) is seen on the right hand side. This particular example would be a regular visitor to North Wales throughout her life until being withdrawn from Longsight depot in July 1984.   **Photo E N Kneale/S Morris collection.**

Holyhead

Right

Based at Holyhead between October and December 1959 for driver training, class 40 number D233 (40033) is seen on number 10 road Old Yard Holyhead just after arrival. Alongside are the first North Wales drivers to be trained on mainline Diesel locomotives. Named "Empress of England" in September 1961, "233" would later gain fame by working the Prince of Wales investiture Royal train to Caernarfon in July 1970, see page 57.

L-R, Driver Charlie Bayliss, operating inspector Fred "Buck" Taylor, Driver George Heydon, inspector E Evans of Chester, driver instructor David Manley Williams, Driver George Owen, Fireman J G Williams, Driver Iorwerth Hughes and Fireman Iorwerth Jones.
Photo John Cave MBE.

Below

Holyhead shed, summer of 1964. Three class 40's await their next turn of duty. Camden allocated D382 (40182) is seen on the left hand side. She would be a regular visitor to the area during her life, remaining based on the "London Midland" throughout. A final allocation to Liverpool Division/Wigan Springs Branch would come as early as September 1968. Withdrawal came from here in June 1982 following just over 20 years service, cutting at Crewe works being completed by April 1984.
Photo E N Kneale/S Morris collection.

Holyhead Drivers

Top left - George Heydon in D233 during driver training in October 1959 **Photo John Cave MBE.**

Middle left - Glyn Williams and Ivor Rowlands. Holyhead, early 1960's.
Bottom left - Brian Evans and Ted Lumley on Holyhead shed, mid 1960's.
Photos E N Kneale/S Morris collection.

Top right - John Jones and 40122, ready to work the 12.45 Holyhead to Euston. August 1st 1987. **Photo Pat Webb.**

Bottom right - Bill Doutch heading across Anglesey during the mid 1960's.
Photo E N Kneale/S Morris collection.

Above
D332 (40132) approaches Holyhead station at the head of a Royal train on August 9th 1965. The complete Royal Family were on board and the full rake is employed, an impressive sight!
Photo E N Kneale/S Morris collection.

Below
D383 (40183) stabled between Black Five locomotives 44773 and 44873 on Holyhead shed during the early 1960's. A true "transition" image!
Photo E N Kneale/Garnedd Jones collection.

Above
The Britannia Bridge fire of May 23rd 1970 resulted in thirteen mainline locomotives being marooned on Anglesey.
Seven class 40's were involved, 219/231/232/233/241/307/390 along with three class 24's, 5034/44/83 and three class 47's,
1724/1851/1940. Class 08's 3004/3174/3175/4137 plus of course the two 01's at the Breakwater were also present. All except
the shunters and class 24's 5034/83 were shipped to Barrow docks from Holyhead on board the "Kingsnorth Fisher" during
mid June 1970, their bogies having first been removed at the CEGB sidings in Valley, see page 76. In this view 233 "Empress
of England" is seen on board the ship concerned, a rare sight indeed!
Photo David Hills collection.

Left
Three class 40's occupy part of
Holyhead shed during the summer
of 1973. Steam has long since
gone but the reminders are all
around.
The four road depot buildings
would be demolished at the end of
1989. Today, a smaller two road
more temporary structure occupies
part of the site for maintaining
multiple units and the odd class 57
locomotive on behalf of Arriva
Trains Wales and Bombardier.
Photo Pat Webb.

Left
40121 seen on the final approach to Holyhead with a down passenger working on April 1st 1977.
The headshunt from the cattle yard can be seen on the right hand side, the water tower in the background.

Below
A rare view of a class 50 at Holyhead, made even more unusual given that it is on a Freightliner working. It is July 23rd 1975 and during a period of a few months when the class was used on 4D62, the 12.20 from Willesden.
Here, 50041 is seen having run around its train and about to propel it into the Freightliner terminal.
Photos Pat Webb.

Right
40105 was the first of twenty class 40's built outside Vulcan Foundry by Robert Stephenson & Hawthorns at Darlington in order to reduce pressure on the main EE production line during a period of intense activity. The number series ran up to D324 (40124) and interestingly the majority of these were amongst the first of the class to be withdrawn when full scale reductions in the fleet size commenced during 1980. Having said that, 40118 went on to be one of the final members to be withdrawn!
In this view, 40105 waits departure from Holyhead platform 2 on the 12.57 summer dated boat train for Euston on August 4th 1979.
Photo Pat Webb.

Above
Another "RSH" built example, 40113 runs around its rake of MK1's alongside Holyhead station during the summer of 1975. Time was running out for this view, within four years the canopy over platform 1 and imposing station hotel buildings dating from June 1880 would have been demolished.
Photo rail-online.co.uk.

Left
August 9th 1980 and Gateshead based 40057 backs on to 1A56, the 13.00 for Euston, on platform 2.
A few years later, this particular member of the class would take on a degree of celebrity when, with 40084, Gateshead depot nominated her for special treatment to cover railtour duties resulting in both locomotives always kept in good external condition.
Photo Pat Webb.

Above
40030 "Scythia" departs Holyhead port on an up Freightliner on August 3rd 1980. Full power would soon be applied, and it was certainly needed, hand sanding sometimes being required on a damp morning to get up the 1 in 75 & 93 gradients past the water tower unaided. This scene has changed completely with the land now occupied by the High Speed Ship (HSS) berth and loading area.

Below
Trains for Anglesey Aluminium needed to visit Holyhead in order for the locomotive to run round the rake before running up to the factory and reversing the load into the complex. In this view, 40076 is seen departing the station with a load of petroleum coke from Immingham on April 15th 1978. Note the Freightliner flat cripple match wagon on the right hand side.
Photos Pat Webb.

Above
January 18th 1981. A view of pioneer class 40, D200/40122 parked at the far west end of Holyhead shed alongside the shed foreman's office. Requests to look around were never turned down! **Photo Peter Hanahoe.**

Below
Prior to the installation of a permanent fuelling point at Holyhead shed following the end of steam operation, a temporary facility was used at the "horse landing" near the station. In this view taken on September 9th 1963, D302 (40102) is seen being fuelled from a road tanker at that location. For reference, the Freightliner cripples in the opposite image are parked in this area. **Photo Barry Wynne.**

Holyhead

Above
40069 approaches Holyhead station at the head of 2D89, the 12.40 Llandudno Junction to Holyhead. This particular example was easily recognisable due to the one off modification it had received to improve access to power unit bedplate oil drainage pipes. The external piping along the solebar associated with this can be clearly seen. Date, June 27th 1982.
Photo Peter Hanahoe.

Below
Longsight based 40097 propels the afternoon Freightliner from Trafford Park into the container terminal at Holyhead during the evening of January 23rd 1982. On May 16th the following year she would become derailed on the approach to Holyhead on exactly the same working, resulting in her withdrawal. This was the only class 40 to actually end its days at Holyhead.
Photo Pat Webb.

Right
40079 waits departure from Holyhead Freightliner terminal on a special up working during the morning of March 13th 1982.

Below
A trio of class 40's are seen stabled on Holyhead shed on Saturday June 11th 1983. 40118 and 40155 would have been regular visitors to the area. Not so common, Healey Mills based 40068 had worked in that morning on 4D52, an 07.09 Freightliner from Basford Hall. She had just six weeks left in service.
Photos Pat Webb.

Right
40143 parked at the east end of Holyhead shed during the summer of 1981. On May 13th of this particular year she was involved in what was probably the most destructive derailment in North Wales for many years. Whilst heading the 4G66 "Liner" to Lawley Street a sandbox fell off the locomotive approaching Llandudno Junction station damaging pointwork. As a result, a number of wagons and their containers were deposited all over the track and platforms at the west end of the station. It was extremely fortunate that no injuries resulted from this.
Photo Pat Webb.

Left
234 (40034) "Accra" on the final approach to Holyhead Freightliner terminal during a summer evening in 1973. Corporate blue now rules and, as can be seen, class 40's dominate the scene in North Wales!
Photo Ron Watson-Jones.

Right
Having worked to Holyhead with 40170 on a Freightliner two days previously, see page 44, 40129 is seen on platform 3 Holyhead station waiting to depart the town on 1A56, the 13.00 to Euston. The date is April 16th 1981 and later that day she would return west heading the 17.25 Crewe to Llandudno. During 1978 40129 been unofficially named "Dracula", something that didn't last for long! **Photo John Stephens.**

Below
We finish off this volume with an overall view of Holyhead as 40183 (see also page 88) is seen working the 14.44 to Manchester Victoria "wrong road" to Valley during engineering works on Sunday June 13th 1982.
This scene has now changed in many ways!
Photo Dave Trains.